Nantes Travel Guide (France)

Discover the most up-to-date and amazing places to explore in Nantes, along with current information and guides on when to go, what to do, and the best places to see.

Hudson Miles

All rights reserved. No part of this publication may be reproduced, distributed, or transmitted in any form or by any means, including photocopying, recording, or other electronic or mechanical methods, without the prior written permission of the publisher, except in the case of brief quotations embodied in critical reviews and certain other noncommercial uses permitted by copyright law.

Copyright © Hudson Miles), (2023).

Table Of Contents

Nantes 101, Homie - A Peek into Nantes's Secrets.

Chapter 2
Talk Like a Local, Holmes - Phrases and Slang Terms for Mixing In.

Chapter 3
Crash Pads in Nantes - Where to Chillax in Style.

Chapter 4
Feasting Frenzy, Buddy - Area Cuisine and Dining Adventures.

Chapter 5
Must-See Nantes: No Joke - Check Out the Coolest Spots.

Chapter 6
Shop 'n' Stop, My Friend - Retail Therapy Nantes-Style.

Chapter 7
Let's Play, Nantes - Leisure Activities for the Fun-Loving Traveler.

Chapter 8

Party Time in Nantes, Y'all - Festivals and Events Galore.

Chapter 9
Route 'n' Roll - Rock Your Travels with Unique Itineraries

Self-Reflection questions

This travel guide provides helpful information. The ideas in the Day trips, Excursions, leisure activities, Itineraries in the city, and Neighboring cities are suggestions. You can craft and explore your vacation in your own style and preparation.

The attractions are listed with their opening hours, starting from the popular ones to the less-known ones. The map in this book provides some knowledge of the city, but the maps on your phone are more detailed. Consider taking screenshots as you walk around with no connection needed. Alternatively, you can contact the tourist office using the addresses and numbers provided in this guide.

If you have more time, explore both popular and less-known attractions mentioned in the notes below. Additionally, if you're interested in shopping, reach out to the stores or reach them through the contact numbers in this book.

For first timers, visiting or contacting the Tourist office, helps you get familiar with the city and it's attractions.

Lastly, try the travel prompts; they help enrich your travel experience and open avenues for personal growth.

The humor in the table of contents is included for an enjoyable reading experience.

Safe Trip....

The Loire-Atlantique department's and the Pays de la Loire region's prefecture's capital is Nantes.

It is the sixth most populated commune in France with little under 300,000 people (more than 600,000 with its urban community).

Nantes, which was built upstream of the Loire Estuary, began as a mediaeval fortress before the dukes of Brittany picked it as their capital and began to construct their castles there in the fourteenth century.

But a very busy commercial port also helped the city to grow quite quickly.

The city was first connected to the Netherlands and the kingdoms of Spain and Portugal by water and river before turning into a starting point for trade to the Americas at the end of the 17th century.

However, the port's heyday coincided with the slave trade in the eighteenth century when ships from Nantes made calls in Africa to embark slaves for the new continent before returning with coffee or sugar.

The city kept growing and gaining inhabitants, and in the nineteenth century, metallurgy and shipbuilding quickly joined the industrialization of the port (refineries, canneries, and biscuit factories).

The city's suburbs were built as a result of the influx of labour, but the city's bourgeois centre was transformed.

The silting up of the Loire was fought with many schemes that were developed in the 20th century, and job losses in industry were countered by growth in tertiary activities.

While preserving its ancient legacy, Nantes cultivates a way of life that keeps it appealing and helps it grow as a major tourist destination, with the ongoing secular argument over whether Nantes should be considered the cultural or administrative capital of Brittany.

Lily of the valley and muscadet white wine represent the soil's best features in the area around it.

Start your tour in the old town, which is a pleasant area to meander through and is home to many historic structures. The magnificent tuffeau interior of the Gothic Cathedral of St. Peter and St. Paul is illuminated by a massive stained glass window honouring the Breton saints that stands 25 metres tall. The tomb of Francis II is situated in this area, in the transept's right arm.

Various half-timbered homes and structures from the 18th and 19th centuries can be seen as you stroll through the historic Le Bouffay neighbourhood. Do you want to go shopping or eat something to satiate your hunger? Visit the Passage Pommeraye, a magnificent covered mall from the 19th century. On its three stories, there are stores and dining establishments. Take note of the stunning glass roof, fluted columns, and wooden and metal staircase!

Nantes has the nickname "City of Dukes" due to the presence of the Castle of the Dukes of Brittany dating back to the 15th century in the centre of the old town. The towers with Breton machicolations and moat are signs that it was originally a stronghold. Among the castle's must-see attractions are the Golden Crown Tower, the well with ducal crown-adorned wrought iron armatures, and the sizable residence built for Francis II with Gothic dormers. The Nantes History Museum is also housed in the castle and provides a unique approach to learn about the city. From Francis I to the present, as well as via industrial Nantes and its current revitalization, you travel a path that is separated into seven sequences.

Go as far as number 86 on the Quai de la Fosse to see several 18th-century homes; they are currently outbuildings for the Durbé palace but were previously a French East India Company warehouse.

There are various green areas in Nantes, including the Japanese garden with its waterfalls on the Ile de Versailles. The Botanical Garden (Jardin des Plantes), which is embellished with water features, is another lovely location to unwind and take in the peace and quiet. It has a diverse collection of cactus and flora from Brittany as well as North America, Asia, and Africa.

Like both history and art? Visit the Fine Arts Museum to see some of the 1,000+ pieces on display, including European paintings from the

13th century to the present. Beautiful collections are available in the Natural History Museum on a variety of topics, including mineralogy, biology, and local fauna. The magnificent skeletons of a fin whale and a basilosaurus isis, the ancestor of the whale and the only example in France, will astound you as you stroll along its walkways.

You will now continue your tour of Nantes by visiting the Ile Feydeau, which was formerly a swampy island. The island was joined to the city in 1926 when the city opted to fill in the River Loire's arms.

The Machines of the Isle (Les Machines de l'île) is a remarkable attraction that can be found on the Ile de Nantes. This display area is sometimes compared to a deft blending of Leonardo da Vinci's creations and the universe of Jules Verne. What you will witness is distinctive: scenarios with animals made of steel and wood that are displayed in an unexpected gallery. Take a trip on the enormous elephant, which has space for roughly fifty people. At the dizzyingly large Marine World Carousel, which is 25 metres tall and 22 metres in diameter, set out to explore the underwater world! All facets of the sea are exhibited inside this mechanical aquarium, from the surface to the deepest caverns, not to mention the seafloor.

Finish your unique trip on the terraces of the workshop, where you can see the amazing animals being built by their designers.

Centre for tourist information
Location: 9 Rue des États, Nantes, France 44000
Opens at 11 a.m.
Phone: +33 892 46 40 44

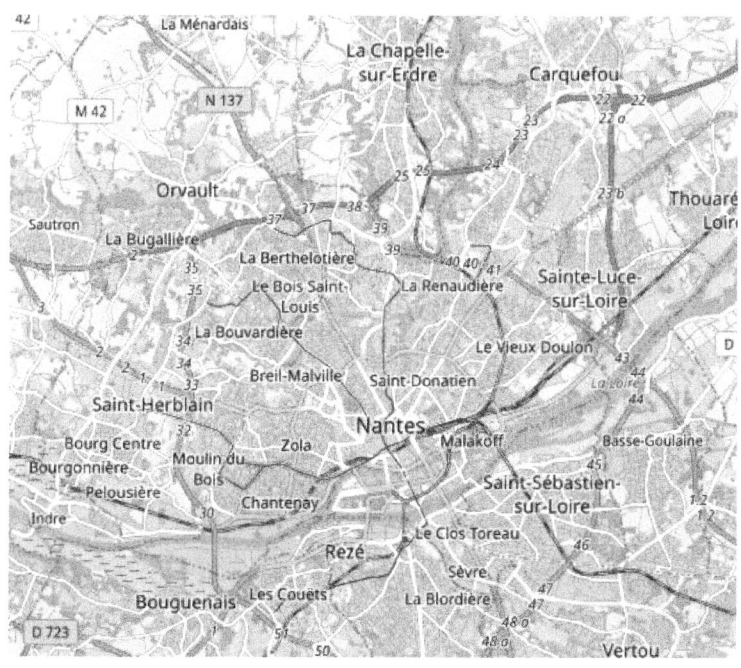

Plan and Pack

Research and Itinerary: Start by learning about the historical places, cultural attractions, and regional activities in Nantes. Create a flexible itinerary that includes must-see sites like the Machines of the Isle of Nantes and the Château des Ducs de Bretagne.

Pick a place to stay that fits your vacation preferences. Nantes has a variety of accommodations, including attractive boutique hotels and inviting bed and breakfasts. It is advised to make reservations in advance, especially during busy times.

Best Time to Visit: Late spring (May to June) or early autumn (September to October) are the best times to visit Nantes. There are less people and milder weather conditions.

What to Bring:

Comfy Clothes: Dress in layers because Nantes weather can change quickly. If you intend to walk throughout the city, you must have comfortable walking shoes.

Make sure your electronic devices are charged by using adapters and chargers. The Type E socket is commonly used by French outlets, therefore carry the necessary adapters.

Language Requirements: Although many people in the area speak English, having a basic understanding of French expressions will improve your experience.

Camera and Journal: Document your memories and the beauty of the city. A journal might serve as a priceless memento of your adventure.

The principal entrance is Nantes Atlantique Airport. As an alternative, think about taking the picturesque high-speed train (TGV) from Paris.
Local transit: Trams and buses are part of Nantes' effective public transit system. Get a Nantes Pass to enjoy popular sights and travel at no additional cost.
 Every detail you require for your trip is included in our revised travel guide. Happy travels!

Chapter 2

Basic french phrases and area slang terms to know before travelling.

Phrases:
- Bonjour - Hello
- Merci - Thank you
- Excusez-moi - Excuse me
- S'il vous plaît - Please
- Au revoir - Goodbye
- Oui - Yes
- Non - No
- Parlez-vous anglais ? - Do you speak English?
- Pouvez-vous m'aider ? - Can you help me?
- Où est... ? - Where is...?
- Combien ça coûte ? - How much does it cost?
- L'addition, s'il vous plaît - The bill, please
- J'aimerais réserver une table - I would like to book a table
- Avez-vous des recommandations ? - Do you have any recommendations?
- Je ne comprends pas - I don't understand
- Pouvez-vous répéter ? - Can you repeat that?
- Quelle est la spécialité locale ? - What is the local specialty?
- L'office de tourisme - Tourist information
- Où puis-je trouver un distributeur automatique ? - Where can I find an ATM?

- Quel est le meilleur moyen de transport ? - What is the best mode of transportation?
- J'ai une réservation - I have a reservation
- Pouvez-vous me recommander un bon restaurant ? - Can you recommend a good restaurant?
- Avez-vous des plats végétariens ? - Do you have vegetarian dishes?
- Où sont les toilettes ? - Where are the toilets?
- C'est délicieux ! - It's delicious!
- Pourriez-vous prendre une photo de moi ? - Could you take a photo of me?
- Où puis-je acheter des souvenirs ? - Where can I buy souvenirs?
- Quel est le mot pour... en français ? - What is the word for... in French?
- J'ai perdu mon chemin - I am lost
- A quelle heure ouvre/ferme... ? - What time does... open/close?
- Puis-je avoir l'addition, s'il vous plaît ? - Can I have the bill, please?
- C'est magnifique ! - It's beautiful!
- J'ai besoin d'un taxi - I need a taxi
- C'est trop cher - It's too expensive
- Pouvez-vous me donner une carte ? - Can you give me a map?
- Est-ce que je peux payer par carte ? - Can I pay by card?
- J'ai une allergie alimentaire - I have a food allergy

- Quelle est la météo aujourd'hui ? - What is the weather like today?

- Je voudrais un café, s'il vous plaît - I would like a coffee, please

- C'est compris ? - Is that understood?

- J'ai réservé une chambre - I have booked a room

- Quel est le meilleur endroit pour voir le coucher de soleil ? - Where is the best place to see the sunset?

- Où puis-je trouver un bureau de change ? - Where can I find a currency exchange?

- Pouvez-vous m'indiquer le chemin vers... ? - Can you show me the way to...?

- Je cherche la gare - I am looking for the train station

- Quel est le mot pour... en français ? - What is the word for... in French?

- Avez-vous des suggestions pour des activités nocturnes ? - Do you have suggestions for nighttime activities?

- Quelle est la meilleure période pour visiter ? - What is the best time to visit?

- Comment puis-je rejoindre le centre-ville ? - How can I get to the city center?

- J'adore cette ville ! - I love this city!

Slang Terms:

- Chouette - Cool or great
- Bouquin - Book (slang for a book)

- Gars/Garçon - Guy or boy
- Nana - Girl or woman
- Bagnole - Car
- Fringues - Clothes
- Taf - Job or work
- Zouz - Girlfriend
- Pote - Friend
- Blé - Money
- Cimer - Thanks (slang)
- Péter un câble - To lose one's temper
- La teuf - Party
- Kiffer - To like or enjoy
- Pote - Friend
- Keuf - Police
- Flipper - To be surprised
- Raide - Drunk
- Pécho - To flirt or pick up
- Barge - Crazy or insane
- Roupiller - To sleep
- Bosser - To work
- En mode - In the mood
- Ouf - Crazy or extreme
- La baraque - House or home
- Chelou - Weird or strange
- Péter la forme - To be in good shape
- Bouffer - To eat
- Bide - Stomach or belly
- Bof - Meh or so-so

Chapter 3

Hotels

Below are recommended hotels to take note of; Consider booking your hotel in advance; Online travel websites like Trivago.com and Booking.com can assist.

- Mercure Nantes Centre - Grand Hôtel
- Location: 4 Rue du Couëdic
- Contact: +33 2 51 82 10 00

Modern chic lodging, free Wi-Fi, restaurant, bar, fitness room. Accessible GPS Zone Pietonne.

- Oceania Hôtel de France Nantes
- Location: 24 Rue Crébillon

- Contact: +33 2 40 73 57 91

Polished 18th-century townhouse, modern quarters, artsy bar, and a touch of historical charm.

- ibis Nantes Centre Tour Bretagne
- Location: 19 Rue Jean Jaurès
- Contact: +33 2 40 35 39 00

Contemporary budget comfort, simple rooms, bar, free Wi-Fi, bistro with a terrace.

- Hôtel Mercure Nantes Centre Passage Pommeraye
- Location: 2 Rue Boileau
- Contact: +33 2 40 48 78 79

Casual comfort with free Wi-Fi, international TV channels, business center, and a library.

- OKKO HOTELS Nantes Château
- Location: 15 Rue de Strasbourg
- Contact: +33 2 52 20 00 70

Contemporary haven, streamlined rooms with Wi-Fi, lounge, sauna, and a delightful breakfast.

- ibis Styles Nantes Centre Gare
- Location: 8 All. Commandant Charcot
- Contact: +33 2 40 74 14 54

Contemporary rooms, relaxed bar, complimentary breakfast, and an unassuming charm.

- Best Western Nantes Hôtel Graslin
  - Location: 1 Rue Piron
  - Contact: +33 2 40 69 72 91

  Understated elegance, complimentary Wi-Fi, and a lounge with a stylish bar.

- Novotel Nantes Centre Bord de Loire
  - Location: 1 Bd des Martyrs Nantais de la Résistance
  - Contact: +33 2 40 47 77 77

  Airy rooms in a casual setting, French restaurant, live music bar, and a kids' playground.

- Hôtel Amiral
  - Location: 26 bis Rue Scribe
  - Contact: +33 2 40 73 56 69

  Unpretentious comfort, contemporary rooms, free WiFi, optional breakfast buffet.

- Hotel Voltaire Opera Nantes Centre
  - Location: 10 Rue Gresset
  - Contact: +33 2 40 73 31 04

  Bright rooms in a classic setting, lounge/bar, conference space, bike storage, and Wi-Fi.

Chapter 4

Restaurants

Try any of the best restaurants for a relaxed and enjoyable time below, along with their contact details.

Lamaccotte
   - Location: 7 Rue Saint-Denis
   - Contact: +33 2 85 37 42 30
    Fine Dining with gourmet French classics like Coq au Vin and Escargot. Relaxed atmosphere.

Pickles
   - Location: 2 Rue du Marais
   - Contact: +33 2 51 84 11 89

Warm bistro serving Ratatouille and Tarte Tatin. Gourmet seasonal French fare.

Restaurant ICI
   - Location: 1 Rue Léon Blum
   - Contact: +33 2 40 48 62 27
   Sleek bistro offering Duck à l'Orange and Crème Brûlée. Creative, seasonal French food.

Le Boudoir - Restaurant Nantes
   - Location: 4 Rue Santeuil
   - Contact: +33 9 81 31 33 33
   French cuisine with global twists, featuring dishes like Bouillabaisse and Beef Bourguignon.

Le Lion et L'agneau
   - Location: 40 Rue Fouré
   - Contact: +33 2 55 10 58 74
   Chic stop for refined French fare, offering Filet Mignon and Sole Meunière.

Cuit Lu Cru
   - Location: 5 Rue Châteaubriand
   - Contact: +33 2 40 74 09 27
   Understated eatery serving reimagined French dishes like Croque Monsieur and Ratatouille.

Les Petits Saints

- Location: 1 Rue Saint-Vincent
- Contact: +33 2 40 20 24 48

Haute French cuisine, no takeaway or delivery. Enjoy dishes like Coquilles Saint-Jacques.

Le Bouchon
- Location: 7 Rue Bossuet
- Contact: +33 2 40 20 08 44

Artfully plated, creative French cuisine with classics like Beef Bourguignon and Ratatouille.

L'Agave
- Location: 11 Rue Léon Blum
- Contact: +33 2 40 47 54 51

Stylish bistro offering fusion fare such as Duck à l'Orange and Tiramisu.

Imagine - Restaurant - Nantes
- Location: 12 Rue Gresset
- Contact: +33 2 40 34 06 11

Chic space for contemporary gastronomy. Sample dishes like Escargot and Crème Brûlée.

La Reine Margot
- Location: 8 Rue de la Juiverie
- Contact: +33 2 40 47 43 85

Intimate setting for French cuisine. Savor dishes like Ratatouille and Bouillabaisse.

Le Fou du Roi
   - Location: 2 Rue Premion
   - Contact: +33 2 40 35 64 64
   Rustic brasserie with castle views. Enjoy classics like Beef Bourguignon and Crêpes Suzette.

Le Square
   - Location: 14 Rue de Jemmapes
   - Contact: +33 2 40 35 98 09
   Modern setting for French & Italian food. Delight in dishes like Quiche Lorraine and Spaghetti Carbonara.

tarte tatin

Chapter 5

Attractions

Below are some of the Attractions in the city, both the popular and the less-known ones, with their operating hours. Visit any of them, depending on your preference.

- Les Machines de l'Île
- Location: Parc des Chantiers, Bd Léon Bureau
- Operating Hours: 10 am–6 pm

   Attraction with giant mechanical animals, a whimsical experience for all.

- Carrousel of the Marine Worlds
- Location: Parc des Chantiers, 2 Bd Léon Bureau
- Operating Hours: 10 am–6 pm

   Perfect attractions for kids and adults, marine-themed carousel delight.

- Jules Verne Museum
- Location: 3 Rue de l'Hermitage
- Operating Hours: 2 pm–6 pm

   Author museum with manuscripts & books, a literary journey awaits.

- Botanical Garden
- Location: Rue Stanislas Baudry
- Operating Hours: 8:30 am–8 pm

19th-century botanical gardens & park, a serene haven of nature.

- Le Grand Éléphant
- Location: 5 Bd Léon Bureau
- Operating Hours: 10 am–6 pm

Amazing and fun place to visit, featuring a grand mechanical elephant.

- Natural History Museum
- Location: 12 Rue Voltaire
- Operating Hours: 10 am–6 pm

200-year-old natural history collection, a journey through Earth's wonders.

- Château des ducs de Bretagne
- Location: 4 Pl. Marc Elder
- Operating Hours: 8:30 am–7 pm

Museum at the seat of the Dukes of Brittany, historical elegance.

- Giant Nantes Sign
- Location: Bd de Stalingrad

Iconic sign, a perfect photo spot to capture Nantes.

- Parc du Grand Blottereau
- Location: 16 Bd Auguste Peneau

- Operating Hours: 8:30 am–10:45 pm
  Landscaped park with tropical planting, a green paradise.

- Parc CRAPA
  - Location: Rue du Pré Salé
  - Operating Hours: Open 24 hours
  Island space with birds & city views, a serene escape.

- Miroir d'eau
  - Location: Pl. Marc Elder
  - Operating Hours: Open 24 hours
  Unique spot, especially enjoyable during hot days, a refreshing view.

- Les Anneaux
  - Location: Quai des Antilles
  - Operating Hours: Open 24 hours
  Modern art installation, a striking sight by the river.

- Cours Cambronne
  - Location: 3 Cr Cambronne
  - Operating Hours: 8:45 am–7:30 pm
  Peaceful promenade lined by mansions, a charming stroll.

- Ile de Versailles
- Location: Quai de Versailles
- Operating Hours: 8:30 am–7:30 pm

    Japanese garden on a small river island, a tranquil escape.

- Oblate Park
- Location: Rue Philippe de Broca
- Operating Hours: 8:45 am–8 pm

    Public green space with a playground, a family-friendly oasis.

- Le Petit Train Touristique de Nantes
- Location: 22 Pl. Saint-Pierre

    Tourist train for exploring Nantes, a delightful city journey.

- Jardin Extraordinaire
- Location: 1 Quai Marquis d'Aiguillon
- Operating Hours: 9 am–6:15 pm

    Garden & waterfall in a former quarry, nature's extraordinary beauty.

- Park Chézine
- Location: Saint-Herblain, France
- Operating Hours: Open 24 hours

    Lots of things for kids and more, a versatile park.

- Jardin Extraordinaire
  - Location: 1 Quai Marquis d'Aiguillon
  - Operating Hours: 9 am–6:15 pm

  Garden & waterfall in a former quarry, nature's extraordinary beauty

Chapter 6

Shopping
Below are some of the best shops in the city.
Try shopping in any of them and bring back some souvenirs home.

- Passage Pommeraye
 - Type: Shopping Mall
 - Address: 20 Pass. Pommeraye
 - Phone: +33 2 40 47 00 26

   19th-century mall with high-end shops, a historic shopping experience.

- Passage Coeur De Nantes

- Type: Shopping Mall
- Address: 10 Rue Santeuil
- Phone: +33 1 53 76 95 53

In-store shopping destination offering diverse retail experiences.

- Centre Commercial Beaulieu
- Type: Shopping Mall
- Address: 1 Bd Général de Gaulle
- Phone: +33 2 40 47 00 26

Spacious retail mall with goods & eats, a one-stop shopping destination.

- Passage Chatelaine
- Type: Shopping Mall
- Address: 11 Rue Scribe

In-store shopping experience in a charming and vibrant passage.

- Maxime
- Type: Shopping Mall
- Address: bis, 2 Pl. François II
- Phone: +33 2 40 48 13 25

In-store shopping destination with a variety of offerings.

- Frip
- Type: Shopping Mall

- Address: 7 Chau. de la Madeleine

Unique in-store shopping experience, offering a curated selection.

- Centre commercial Paridis
- Type: Shopping Mall
- Address: 10 Rte de Paris
- Phone: +33 2 40 93 97 20

In-store shopping with the option for in-store pick-up.

- SEGECE
- Type: Shopping Mall
- Address: Centre Commercial Beaulieu, Bd Général de Gaulle
- Phone: +33 2 40 47 00 26

In-store shopping experience with a focus on quality offerings.

- Centre commercial Carrefour Nantes La Beaujoire
- Type: Shopping Mall
- Address: Nantes, France
- Phone: +33 2 41 32 87 96

Large shopping center with a supermarket, offering diverse choices.

- Galeries Lafayette

- Type: Clothing Store
- Address: 2-20 Rue de la Marne
- Phone: +33 2 40 99 82 12

In-store shopping with in-store pick-up and delivery options.

- The Wizard's Shop
- Type: Gift Shop
- Address: Passage Pommeraye Angle galerie centrale et galerie Régnier, niveau 1
- Phone: +33 1 85 09 74 50

In-store shopping for magical and unique gifts.

- Quater Back
- Type: Shopping Mall
- Address: Centre Commercial Beaulieu, Bd Général de Gaulle
- Phone: +33 2 40 75 61 81

In-store shopping destination with a focus on diverse products.

- Picture store nantes
- Type: Clothing Store
- Address: Pass. Pommeraye
- Phone: +33 2 51 17 87 58

In-store shopping for clothing with a diverse selection.

Chapter 7

Leisure Activities

Below are more activities and Excursions to get involved in.

- The Nantes City Pass costs €27. With the City Pass, which provides free entry to important sites, tours, and public transport for 24, 48, or 72 hours, you may fully experience Nantes' artistic and cultural offerings. 370 metres from Nantes's centre.

- Tour of an artisanal salmon smokehouse:

In order to find an artisanal salmon smokehouse founded in 1984, travel 25 kilometres from Nantes. Learn the craft of smoking fish, particularly salmon from the chilly waters of northern Europe. Watch as these Scottish or Irish fish of the highest calibre are expertly prepared by hand.

- Legendia Parc:

Cost: 23 euros Travel 32 kilometres from Nantes to the "Pays de Retz" and visit Legendia Parc, a legendary place with a distinctive theme in France. This conserved park, which covers 33 hectares, enchants visitors with its magical features. Create priceless experiences in the charm of Legendia Parc with family or friends.

Chapter 8

Festivals and events

Attending some of the events listed below in the city or nearby can help make your travelling memorable.

- La Folle Journée in Nantes, which will take place in February 2024. La Folle Journée, one of Europe's greatest classical music festivals, draws crowds with outstanding performances right in the centre of Nantes.

- Voyage à Nantes Trail

July/August 2024 in Nantes - Wander around Nantes on the Voyage à Nantes trail, a lyrical and artistic trip crisscrossing the city and fostering a singular and immersive cultural experience.

- Les Escales

Scheduled for Saint-Nazaire in August 2024. Experience a fusion of traditional and modern global music at the Les Escales festival, which takes place in Saint-Nazaire, a bustling city close to Nantes.

- Gois Run

Take part in the thrilling Gois Run in July 2024 at Beauvoir-sur-Mer, close to Nantes, which offers an adrenaline-pumping adventure amidst stunning coastal settings.

- La Gacilly Photo Festival: held in La Gacilly in July, August, September, and October 2024. Discover La Gacilly, the largest outdoor photo event in France, where photographers converge to take in eye-catching visual narratives amidst breathtaking scenery.

- Hellfest

Scheduled for June 2024 in Clisson. At Hellfest in Clisson, close to Nantes, unleash the power of heavy metal as the event turns into a haven for devoted fans looking for an exhilarating musical experience.

- New Beaujolais Festival:
- November 16–19, all throughout France - Celebrate the release of the new Beaujolais wine with joy and tradition at the New Beaujolais Festival, a national celebration showcasing French vineyards.

- European Museum Night will take place on May 20, 2024, in France. During European Museum Night, join a celebratory evening of discovery in museums all over France. Cultural treasures come to life, providing a fascinating and engaging experience.

- Rendez-vous aux Jardins Garden Festival
Everywhere in France in June 2024, Rendez-vous aux Jardins brings together nature and plant lovers to celebrate the beauty and tranquilly of France's many green spaces.

Chapter 9

Itinerary

Below is a detailed 6 days Itinerary suggestions, you can adjust it based on your preference and timing.

- Day 1: Examine the Ancient Heart

- Morning: Get a sense of the past of Nantes by starting the day at the Château des Ducs de Bretagne.
- In the afternoon, have lunch at a classic French bistro in Nantes' Bouffay Quarter. Discover the boutique stores and crowded streets.
- In the evening, take a leisurely boat ride along the Erdre River in Nantes and stroll around the riverfront while dining.

- Day 2: Culture and the Arts

- In the morning, take in the remarkable fusion of engineering and art at Les Machines de l'île (Nantes).
- Afternoon: Have lunch nearby and explore the Lu Tower (Nantes), a reminder of the area's industrial past.
- In the evening, see a show at Le Lieu Unique (Nantes), a cultural hub housed in a former biscuit factory.

Day Three: Island of Gardens and Machines

- In the morning, visit Les Machines de l'île again to see any displays you might have missed.
- In the afternoon, spend some time relaxing at the lovely botanical garden Jardin des Plantes in Nantes.
- In the evening, unwind at a neighbouring café or eatery while taking in the atmosphere of the city.

Day 4: Shopping and contemporary architecture
- Morning: Discover the cultural spaces and the island of Nantes' cutting-edge architecture.
- In the afternoon, indulge in some retail therapy at the famed shopping arcade Passage Pommeraye (Nantes).
- In the evening, eat dinner at a hip eatery in the city.

Day 5: The Maritime Heritage of Nantes
- In the morning, visit the Navibus in Nantes and take a Loire River boat excursion.
- In the afternoon, visit the Machines of the Isle Shipyard in Nantes to see how remarkable creations are built.
- In the evening, eat at a riverfront seafood restaurant.

Day 6: Full-Day Day Trip to Clisson: Visit Clisson, a charming village close to Nantes noted for its Italian-style architecture and castle ruins.
- In the evening, travel back to Nantes for a final dinner at a quaint neighbourhood eatery.

Self-Reflection questions

Below are some personal questions, answering them can help enrich your travel experience. Safe trip

Travelling to Nantes, France provides an opportunity for personal development and self-discovery in addition to providing an opportunity to explore a dynamic city. Self-reflection exercises are essential for improving your travel expertise. They provide you the chance to delve more deeply into your feelings, perspectives, and the effect the journey has had on your own growth.

Prior to departure:
1. Expectations and anticipation:
 - What particular features of Nantes are you looking forward to seeing the most, and what expectations do you now have?

_____
_____
_____
_____
_____

What personal objectives, whether they pertain to cultural awareness, leisure, or personal enrichment, do you aim to accomplish during your time in Nantes?

3. Cultural Intelligence: How well-versed are you in Nantes' intricacies of culture and history? What actions can you take in advance to improve your cultural sensitivity?

_____
_____
_____

4. Openness to New Experiences: Consider how comfortable you are deviating from your regular routine. What hobbies or experiences outside of your comfort zone are you willing to try?

_____
_____
_____
_____
_____
_____
_____

5. Mindful Presence: As you set out on your adventure, think about your thinking. How can you make an effort to be mindful and in the moment when visiting Nantes so that you can completely savour and appreciate each moment?

_____
_____
_____

_____
_____
_____
_____
_____

After a trip:
1. Remarkable Occasions: What particular experiences or moments from your trip to Nantes will you treasure the most, and how have they shaped your individual memories?

_____
_____
_____
_____
_____
_____
_____
_____

2. The Effect on Perspectives: What new insights have you gained from visiting Nantes, whether they be in regards to various cultures, historical significance, or personal development?

_____

_____
_____
_____
_____
_____
_____
_____

3. Unexpected Discoveries: - Consider any surprising findings or learnings you made along the way. What new insights have these discoveries given you about who you are and how the world works?

_____
_____
_____
_____
_____
_____
_____

4. Appreciation of Culture: - Think about how your understanding of cultures has changed. What aspects of Nantes culture have stayed with you and how might they affect your outlook on the future?

Inclusion in Everyday Life: How do you intend to apply the knowledge, sentiments, and fresh insights from Nantes to your everyday life? What actions can you do to make sure your trip experience has an everlasting effect?

Note:

Note:

Note:

Note: